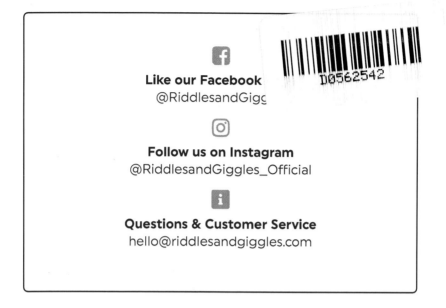

Like our Facebook
@RiddlesandGig...

Follow us on Instagram
@RiddlesandGiggles_Official

Questions & Customer Service
hello@riddlesandgiggles.com

Would You Rather Book for Kids Easter Edition

by Riddles and Giggles™

www.riddlesandgiggles.com

RIDDLES AND GIGGLES
FREE BONUS

Get your FREE book download

Jokes & Would You Rather for Kids.
Easter Edition

- ⊘ Contains a collection of Egg-cellent Easter Jokes and Would You Rather Easter-Themed Questions

- ⊘ More endless giggles and entertainment for the whole family.

Claim your FREE book at
www.riddlesandgiggles.com/easter

Or scan with your phone to get your free download

TABLE OF CONTENTS

Hi there!

Would You Rather Book for Kids Easter Edition is a collection of funny scenarios, wacky choices and hilarious situations to choose from.

Some questions might be tough because they are asking you to choose between two good things, such as picking out your favorite candy. But some questions will be tough because you have to choose between two gross options!

Make sure you take your time and think about which option you prefer—and the reason why!

These questions are fun for all ages and are sure to inspire fun conversations with the whole family.

How to Play

Would You Rather is a fun game that can be played in a group or by yourself.

You are not allowed to answer "neither" or "both"—**you must choose an** answer!

Remember, there are no right or wrong answers; the aim of the book is to have fun.

If you're playing in a group, ask a question and let everyone think of their answer. As you go around and hear everyone's answer, ask them why they made their choice. Sometimes hearing the reasons behind an answer is just as fun as asking the questions.

If you take turns, make sure everyone gets a chance to read a question from each section because some are much sillier than others!

Would you rather play for fun or keep score?

Level up your game so you can determine a winner! This game is tons of fun on its own, but you can also choose to play for points. Adding a layer of guessing gives you a chance to discover who knows the players best. Plus, you'll get a chance to be crowned the winner!

Label each option as A or B. Give players a pencil and piece of paper so they can write down their pick. Before the other players say their answer out loud, the person who read the question will try to guess each player's choice. If they get one right, they get a point! If you play this way, make sure to go around the room, giving every player a chance to be the reader and earn points. Add up all the points at the end of the game and see who knows everyone the best and will be crowned the winner!

This book is a fun game and a great way to learn about each other. But above all, everyone will have tons of fun and there will be plenty of giggles!

PSST...you can also color in the Easter pictures and use this book as a coloring book AND a Would You Rather question book!

1

EASTER BUNNY

➜ Would you rather meet the Easter Bunny or meet your favorite celebrity?

➜ Would you rather hide eggs like the Easter Bunny does or deliver presents like Santa Claus does?

➜ Would you rather grow bunny ears or grow a bunny tail?

➜ Would you rather the Easter Bunny bring one small Easter basket for yourself or bring one huge Easter basket to share with all your friends?

➜ Would you rather be friends with a talking bunny or be friends with a talking squirrel?

→ Would you rather dress up as the Easter Bunny for a week or dress up as a chicken for a week?

→ Would you rather be covered from head to toe in bunny fur or have bunny claws instead of fingernails?

→ Would you rather get a small Easter basket overflowing with goodies or get a huge basket that just has a few things?

→ Would you rather search outside for 30 eggs that are hard to find or see 100 eggs right out in the open?

→ Would you rather spend an entire month hopping like the Easter Bunny or waddling like a duck?

➡️ Would you rather the Easter Bunny bring you a new puppy as a pet or bring you a baby chick for a pet?

➡️ Would you rather the Easter Bunny hide eggs outside in your yard or hide eggs inside of your house?

➡️ Would you rather have to write an essay about the Easter Bunny for a grade or have to make up a song about the Easter Bunny and sing it in front of the entire school?

➡️ Would you rather live down in the Easter Bunny's burrow or live high up in a bird's nest?

➔ Would you rather have chicken feathers or Easter Bunny fur instead of skin?

➔ Would you rather the Easter Bunny come and bring you candy once a month or Santa Claus come and bring you presents twice a year?

➔ Would you rather the Easter Bunny hide eggs filled with candy or filled with money?

➔ Would you rather record yourself dressed as an egg singing a song to post on YouTube, where it will stay forever and anyone in the world can see it, or dress up as the Easter Bunny and dance on live TV where only your neighborhood will see it?

→ Would you rather travel with the Easter Bunny by riding on his back or travel by hanging on to his ears like they were a horse's reins?

→ Would you rather be the Easter Bunny's assistant and earn $20 but only work every Easter Sunday or be the Tooth Fairy's assistant and earn $100 by working every night?

→ Would you rather the Easter Bunny hide 100 eggs for you to find or just give you 50 chocolate eggs in your basket?

→ Would you rather not get any candy or treats from the Easter Bunny or have to pick up your dog's poop on every walk for the rest of your life?

→ Would you rather be friends with only the Easter Bunny or keep all your real friends and never see the Easter Bunny in person?

→ Would you rather the Easter Bunny send you an email or draw a picture for you?

→ Would you rather the Easter Bunny bring you enough candy to last the whole year or bring you the newest toy you have been wanting to get for a long time?

→ Would you rather find out that the Easter Bunny has the softest fur in the world but smells like rotten milk or find out that the Easter Bunny has porcupine quills but smells like fresh baked cookies?

→ Would you rather take a selfie with the Easter Bunny or get a letter from the Easter Bunny signed with his autograph?

→ Would you rather follow the Easter Bunny everywhere for one night or find $10 on the ground?

→ Would you rather send the Easter Bunny on a vacation to the beach or to the mountains after he completes his Easter duties?

→ Would you rather feed the Easter Bunny carrots or lettuce?

WOULD YOU RATHER FOR KIDS EASTER EDITION

➡ Would you rather the Easter Bunny take one bite out of every piece of candy he leaves for you or for him to leave you no candy at all?

➡ Would you rather have an extra finger on each hand or have a bunny tail on your bottom?

➡ Would you rather have to keep your hair buzzed short or have hair like a poufy Easter Bunny tail on top of your head?

➡ Would you rather have a bunny nose instead of your nose or a chicken beak instead of your mouth?

→ Would you rather see special pastel fireworks on Easter night or go to an Easter parade?

→ Would you rather have to wear a crazy clown wig on your head or an Easter Bunny tail on your bottom for the rest of your life?

→ Would you rather the Easter Bunny hide eggs up high where you need a ladder to grab them or down low where you have to lie on your belly to find them?

→ Would you rather be able to talk to the Easter Bunny over the phone or see him in person but not understand him when he talks?

→ Would you rather be able to hop around like the Easter Bunny or slither around on the ground like a snake?

→ Would you rather meet the Easter Bunny or meet the Tooth Fairy?

→ Would you rather the Easter Bunny be as tiny as a hamster or as big as a Tyrannosaurus Rex?

EASTER
CANDY AND FOOD

→ Would you rather get an Easter egg filled with M&M's candies or Skittles candies?

→ Would you rather get a bag full of black licorice jelly beans in your Easter basket or a pack of red licorice in your Easter basket?

→ Would you rather find eggs that have chocolate inside or find eggs that have toys inside?

→ Would you rather eat a small bunny made of solid chocolate or a large chocolate bunny that was hollow?

→ Would you rather get an Easter basket with jelly beans and fruity candy inside or an Easter basket with chocolate candy inside?

→ Would you rather eat ham or turkey at Easter dinner?

→ Would you rather eat five deviled eggs or 10 scrambled eggs?

→ Would you rather have to do all your chores or search for 1,000 jelly beans in a field of grass?

→ Would you rather have to eat an entire chocolate bunny that was two feet tall by yourself or eat an entire pizza by yourself?

→ Would you rather have to wear clothes with Peeps stuck all over them or clothes with jelly beans stuck all over them?

➡ Would you rather have to jump in a pool filled with soda or a pool filled with chocolate milkshake?

➡ Would you rather have a chocolate mustache for a day or a jelly bean stuck in your ear for a day?

➡ Would you rather get gooey marshmallow Peeps stuck all over your fingers or melted chocolate in your hair?

➡ Would you rather be invited to the White House for Easter dinner or invite your favorite celebrity to your house for Easter dinner?

➡ Would you rather be allergic to fruity candy or allergic to chocolate?

➡ Would you rather your household has no power on Easter or has no food on Easter?

➡ Would you rather wear a sign to school that lists all the food you ate on Easter or a sign that lists all the candy you got in your Easter basket?

➡ Would you rather eat the green part of five carrots or eat five chocolate-covered dog treats?

→ Would you rather eat one dozen chocolate-covered jalapeno peppers or one dozen chocolate-covered worms on Easter?

→ Would you rather unwrap 500 pieces of candy or peel 50 hard-boiled eggs?

→ Would you rather time travel to an Easter lunch 100 years ago or time travel to an Easter lunch 100 years into the future?

→ Would you rather eat a piece of Easter pie topped with toenail clippings or a piece of Easter pie that has ear wax mixed into the filling?

➜ Would you rather eat only candy the whole day on Easter or not be able to eat any candy for the next month?

➜ Would you rather eat candy that is shaped like a rabbit's tail or shaped like a pig's hoof?

➜ Would you rather get no candy in your Easter basket or have no Internet access on Easter day?

➜ Would you rather eat an Easter lunch that your dog drooled on or an Easter lunch someone poured out a bottle of ketchup on?

→ Would you rather decorate Easter cookies or dye and decorate Easter eggs?

→ Would you rather eat gummy bears or jelly beans from your Easter basket?

→ Would you rather eat a hard-boiled egg in one big bite or crack a raw egg on your head?

→ Would you rather bake an apple pie to eat or make a mud pie for fun?

→ Would you rather eat 20 chocolate eggs or 20 marshmallow Peeps in one hour on Easter?

➡️ Would you rather get 10 candy bars that have one bite taken out of each of them or get five candy bars that are not your favorite kind?

➡️ Would you rather eat cake or pie for dessert on Easter?

➡️ Would you rather eat ice cream outside on a cold Easter day or take a bite of a brownie as soon as it comes out of the oven?

➡️ Would you rather eat Peanut Butter M&M's or Reese's Peanut Butter Cups on Easter?

➡️ Would you rather bake cupcakes or a chocolate cake for Easter dessert?

→ Would you rather eat an Easter candy that tastes like broccoli or like fish?

→ Would you rather eat one giant chocolate egg or one giant jelly bean?

→ Would you rather share your Easter candy with your friends and be able to share theirs or keep all your candy for yourself?

→ Would you rather get a Snickers candy bar or a Milky Way candy bar in your Easter basket?

→ Would you rather eat chocolate eggs or pancakes for Easter breakfast?

WOULD YOU RATHER FOR KIDS EASTER EDITION

➜ Would you rather get an extra day off school after Easter or get two extra chocolate bunnies in your Easter basket?

➜ Would you rather eat carrots as the only vegetable for the rest of your life or never eat chocolate again?

➜ Would you rather get one big chocolate bunny or 10 small chocolate eggs in your Easter basket?

➜ Would you rather cook hard-boiled eggs or scrambled eggs for your entire family on Easter morning?

➡ Would you rather have an Easter basket that magically produces 10 chocolate eggs each day or never have homework again?

➡ Would you rather help cook Easter dinner or help clean up afterward?

➡ Would you rather smash a raw egg in your bare hand or smash a plastic egg filled with mayonnaise in your bare hand?

➡ Would you rather eat one whole onion or 30 whole carrots at Easter lunch?

➡ Would you rather eat at home or go to a restaurant for Easter dinner?

➡ Would you rather the sides at Easter lunch be only fruits or only vegetables?

WOULD YOU RATHER FOR KIDS EASTER EDITION

→ Would you rather juggle or play catch using raw eggs?

→ Would you rather use an entire jar of jam on one Easter roll or never eat another roll?

→ Would you rather brush your teeth with mayonnaise instead of toothpaste or drink a cup of sour milk with your breakfast on Easter morning?

→ Would you rather have no meat for Easter lunch or no bread?

→ Would you rather have the entire Easter dinner be served cold or hot?

→ Would you rather eat beans that have a hair in them or macaroni and cheese that has a toenail on them?

→ Would you rather throw out half of your Easter meal or have to eat two plates full?

→ Would you rather drink soda with your Easter dinner or drink iced tea with your Easter dinner?

→ Would you rather juggle jelly beans or eat Easter eggs?

→ Would you rather be able to drink only water or to eat only salad on Easter?

➜ Would you rather eat no cheese or no chocolate on Easter?

➜ Would you rather eat pasta or Chinese food on Easter?

➜ Would you rather dip everything from your Easter meal in ketchup or mustard?

➜ Would you rather have pizza or tacos for Easter breakfast?

➜ Would you rather eat nothing sweet or nothing salty on Easter?

➜ Would you rather eat French fries or onion rings on Easter?

➜ Would you rather have macaroni and cheese or spaghetti on Easter?

➜ Would you rather have biscuits or rolls for Easter?

➜ Would you rather have no candy or no cake on Easter?

➜ Would you rather eat a Lunchables or a frozen pizza for Easter dinner?

➜ Would you rather add onions or pickles to all of the food on your Easter plate?

→ Would you rather put honey or jam on your Easter rolls?

→ Would you rather eat tater tots with your Easter dinner or eat mashed potatoes with your Easter dinner?

→ Would you rather give up candy or cake until next Easter?

→ Would you rather eat pizza or hot dogs for every meal until next Easter?

→ Would you rather eat broccoli-chip cookies or carrot ice cream for Easter dessert?

→ Would you rather have to eat your entire Easter meal with only a spoon or have to eat your entire Easter meal with only a knife?

→ Would you rather have rice as a side with your Easter meal or noodles as a side with your Easter meal?

→ Would you rather put a dollop of mayonnaise or ranch dressing on your dessert?

→ Would you rather eat an entire lemon or lime before Easter dinner?

→ Would you rather eat cupcakes for Easter breakfast or pancakes for Easter dinner?

→ Would you rather eat boiled snails or fried grasshoppers for Easter lunch?

→ Would you rather eat a scoop of cookie or brownie batter before you bake them for Easter treats?

→ Would you rather put cheese or peanut butter on your Easter roll?

→ Would you rather eat a cricket or have to eat all of your Easter candy at once?

→ Would you rather eat a stick of butter or drink a cup of ranch dressing before Easter dinner?

→ Would you rather eat steak or fish for Easter dinner?

→ Would you rather eat a bagel or a donut for breakfast on Easter?

→ Would you rather eat Easter leftovers for two weeks straight or not have any food left over at all?

→ Would you rather eat your Easter meal with your hands or eat your Easter meal with your feet?

→ Would you rather eat all the eggs you find or decorate all the eggs you find?

→ Would you rather eat only hot food or only cold food until next Easter?

→ Would you rather eat only healthy foods or junk foods for Easter dinner?

→ Would you rather eat a granola bar or a candy bar on Easter?

EASTER CANDY AND FOOD

→ Would you rather eat Triscuits or Wheat Thins on Easter?

→ Would you rather eat Cheetos or Doritos on Easter?

→ Would you rather eat chips and dip or popcorn on Easter?

→ Would you rather eat ice cream or frozen yogurt on Easter?

→ Would you rather eat sugary cereal or donuts for breakfast on Easter?

→ Would you rather eat butter popcorn or cheese popcorn while you watch an Easter movie?

→ Would you rather eat Goldfish or Cheez-Its for an Easter snack?

→ Would you rather bake brownies that are topped with Easter sprinkles or make pretty pastel-colored Rice Krispies Treats for Easter dessert?

→ Would you rather dip a pretzel or corn dog in mustard on Easter?

→ Would you rather eat carrot sticks or celery on Easter?

→ Would you rather eat Pirate's Booty or Cheese Balls on Easter?

→ Would you rather eat a graham cracker that is topped with peanut butter or a graham cracker that is topped with marshmallow fluff on Easter?

→ Would you rather cook a s'more over the campfire or eat a scoop of ice cream on Easter?

→ Would you rather eat a fruit roll-up or gummy worms on Easter?

→ Would you rather eat Oreos or bake sugar cookies for Easter?

→ Would you rather eat the whole cake at Easter dinner or never be able to eat cake again?

➡ Would you rather your entire Easter meal be foods that are shaped like circles or foods that are shaped like squares?

➡ Would you rather get a grape stuck in your ear or a pea stuck in your nose on Easter?

➡ Would you rather take a bite of moldy bread or eat a rotten potato on Easter?

➡ Would you rather not use a fork for Easter dinner or have to use a fork for everything you eat, even candy?

➡ Would you rather have fingernails that tasted like chips or toenails that tasted like chocolate?

→ Would you rather cook your whole Easter dinner in the microwave or only serve food that does not have to be cooked?

→ Would you rather have to eat egg-shaped food for the rest of your life or never eat an actual egg ever again?

→ Would you rather eat an entire uncooked cake or drink an entire tub of melted ice cream for Easter dessert?

→ Would you rather the clouds always be made of cotton candy or have it rain chocolate drops on Easter?

EASTER FUN

→ Would you rather fly a kite while holding a raw egg in one hand or swing on a swing while balancing a raw egg on your lap?

→ Would you rather go on an Easter egg hunt or a scavenger hunt?

→ Would you rather hide eggs for someone else to hunt or search for the eggs someone has hidden for you?

→ Would you rather hunt for Easter eggs on a rocky mountain or a sandy beach?

→ Would you rather it snows while you are hunting for Easter eggs or be so hot you end up drenched in sweat?

→ Would you rather stand up in front of your whole school and do the Chicken Dance or the Bunny Hop?

→ Would you rather search for 100 Easter eggs that each had a quarter inside, or search for 20 Easter eggs that each had $1 inside?

→ Would you rather get a fluffy live chick for Easter or a tasty marshmallow Peep chick?

→ Would you rather dye and decorate 100 Easter eggs or plant 20 flower seeds?

EASTER FUN

➜ Would you rather carry around one uncooked egg for a week or 50 plastic eggs?

➜ Would you rather have flowers growing from your head instead of hair or Easter grass growing instead of eyelashes?

➜ Would you rather your body become a huge plastic Easter egg, or your teeth become jelly beans?

➜ Would you rather wear an Easter basket as a hat for a week or wear plastic Easter eggs on each of your fingers for a week?

➜ Would you rather all of your clothes be in shades of Easter pastels or all of them be in bring spring colors?

WOULD YOU RATHER FOR KIDS EASTER EDITION

➜ Would you rather your teacher gives you a piece of candy for Easter or gives you a night with no homework assigned?

➜ Would you rather sing a silly Easter song in front of your entire school or record a video of you dancing to post on YouTube?

➜ Would you rather know how to say "Happy Easter" in 100 different languages or know the answer to 100 Easter trivia questions?

➜ Would you rather have no voice on Easter day or sing everything you say on Easter day?

→ Would you rather your house has no Internet on Easter or you have to use the bathroom outside on Easter?

→ Would you rather have a persistent cough or hiccups on Easter?

→ Would you rather not be able to talk at all during Easter lunch or have to say every thought that crosses your mind out loud?

→ Would you rather hide 100 plastic eggs for your family to find or dye 100 hard-boiled eggs for Easter decorations?

WOULD YOU RATHER FOR KIDS EASTER EDITION

→ Would you rather spend your entire Easter celebration with your family while wearing your shoes on the wrong feet or while wearing your shirt on backward?

→ Would you rather let a bunny scratch you or a chick peck you?

→ Would you rather kiss a frog or kiss a pig on Easter?

→ Would you rather spend Easter being invisible or being silent?

→ Would you rather have a pet bunny that talks or a pet chick that lays chocolate eggs?

→ Would you rather sing "Here Comes Peter Cottontail" or "Five Little Bunnies" over and over on Easter day?

→ Would you rather spend Easter outside drawing with sidewalk chalk or blowing bubbles?

→ Would you rather get pecked by a chicken or chased by a goose on Easter?

→ Would you rather peep like a chick when you try to talk or hop like a bunny when you try to walk?

→ Would you rather run as fast as you can to find Easter eggs or look carefully?

→ Would you rather ride a unicorn or Pegasus for a day on Easter?

→ Would you rather write an Easter poem or read an Easter poem?

→ Would you rather have an Easter party at school with all of your classmates and your teacher or have an Easter party at home with just your family and no friends invited?

➡ Would you rather hold a baby bunny or a baby chick?

➡ Would you rather have to wear an Easter Bunny costume or a Santa Claus suit for gym class and recess?

➡ Would you rather do an Easter-themed science project or an art project?

➡ Would you rather a bird fly into your house or a bat fly into your house on Easter?

➡ Would you rather be an Easter superhero who delivered candy to everyone in your city or hide Easter eggs for everyone in your city?

→ Would you rather spend all of Easter with eight little ducklings following you everywhere or a swarm of butterflies flying above your head?

→ Would you rather spend Easter wrapped in a spiderweb or dressed as a toilet paper mummy?

→ Would you rather have a tarantula on each shoulder during Easter dinner or eat a chocolate-covered beetle for dessert?

→ Would you rather put on a puppet show or a shadow puppet show on Easter, featuring a bunny and a chick?

→ Would you rather sleep on a bed of Easter grass or walk across a floor of plastic eggs?

→ Would you rather everyone you meet on Easter think you are the smartest person ever or the funniest person ever?

→ Would you rather play hide and seek or hunt for eggs on Easter?

→ Would you rather play baseball using plastic eggs as balls or Easter baskets as bats?

→ Would you rather spend all day on Easter being five years older than you are now or two years younger?

→ Would you rather draw the best Easter picture ever or sing the best Easter song ever?

➜ Would you rather be able to cast spells or have a superpower on Easter?

➜ Would you rather sail a boat or ride in a hang glider on Easter?

➜ Would you rather lick the trash can after everyone threw out their candy wrappers or lick the bathroom floor after the whole family came over for an Easter celebration?

➜ Would you rather have a robot that does anything you ask it to do during Easter day or a magic carpet that flies you around on Easter day?

→ Would you rather see fireworks on Easter or not see fireworks for any holiday all year?

→ Would you rather fly a kite while you are riding a scooter on Easter or dribble a basketball while you are riding a bike on Easter?

→ Would you rather be on the same team as your family or as your friends when you play baseball on Easter?

→ Would you rather have to hop around like a bunny for all of Easter or only be able to walk backward?

➜ Would you rather be able to speak a secret language no one but your friends can understand or create a special holiday that only your friends know about?

➜ Would you rather meet a famous singer or a famous actor on Easter?

➜ Would you rather get a chance to design the toy of your dreams or always get any candy you ask for?

➜ Would you rather be able to control the weather on Easter or be able to plan the menu for your Easter meal?

➜ Would you rather spend Easter on the Moon or on Mars?

→ Would you rather not be able to watch TV on Easter or not be able to use the Internet?

→ Would you rather be able to fly in the sky on Easter or be able to swim in the deep sea with your eyes open?

→ Would you rather have a hand as big as a dinner plate forever or only be able to use your hands for dinner plates on Easter?

→ Would you rather have to loudly say the name of the person talking to you every time someone spoke to you or have to do cartwheels in and out of the room on Easter morning?

➡ Would you rather spend Easter day with wings you cannot fly with or have gills you cannot breathe underwater with?

➡ Would you rather eat a beetle with Easter dinner or get stung by a bee on Easter morning?

➡ Would you rather be able to dye your hair a pastel color for Easter or have to wear grass as your hair all day?

➡ Would you rather live in a mansion with your entire family on every Easter day or live in your own apartment (and have to pay rent and bills!) for the whole year?

➡ Would you rather have five brothers or five sisters to share your Easter candy with?

➡ Would you rather invite an Olympic athlete over to play Easter games with your family or invite the President of the United States to eat Easter dinner with your whole family?

➡ Would you rather drink a cup of hot sauce or eat a whole jar of mayonnaise on Easter?

➡ Would you rather not listen to any music on Easter or not watch any movies or TV shows for the whole month of Easter?

➡ Would you rather get a new shirt for Easter or a new pair of shoes?

➡ Would you rather get a snowstorm on Easter or get a week of no homework from school?

➡ Would you rather sweat honey on Easter or smell like a skunk when you get sweaty?

➡ Would you rather have to shovel snow after an Easter blizzard or mow the grass on Easter?

➡ Would you rather learn how to play an Easter song on the piano or the guitar?

→ Would you rather not be able to eat any of your Easter candy for an entire week or not be able to watch any TV shows during that time?

→ Would you rather drive in a car to a friend's house on Easter or fly across the country to a relative's house?

→ Would you rather be able to freeze time and have Easter last as long as you want or be able to skip time ahead to live any one day in the future?

→ Would you rather be trapped in a room with a swarm of bees for the entire day on Easter or stand still while a chicken pecked you for two hours?

→ Would you rather spend time on Easter in a kiddie pool of chocolate pudding or an Olympic-size swimming pool of strawberry ice cream?

→ Would you rather have a police officer show up at your Easter celebration or have the fire department come by?

→ Would you rather play paintball or laser tag on Easter?

→ Would you rather have Easter lunch as a picnic in the park with ants or a picnic on the beach with sand?

WOULD YOU RATHER FOR KIDS EASTER EDITION

➜ Would you rather have to crow like a rooster every morning when you wake up or wiggle your nose like a bunny all day, every day?

➜ Would you rather have to get dressed up in fancy clothes for Easter or be wearing your pajamas when your entire family came over?

➜ Would you rather drive to your relative's house for Easter dinner in a convertible on a cold day or eat your entire Easter meal on a moving double-decker bus?

➜ Would you rather have to wear only your bathing suit for the whole day on Easter or have to wear long pants and a winter coat?

➡ Would you rather have to go see the doctor on Easter or have to go to the dentist?

➡ Would you rather invite Spider-Man or Superman over to your house for your Easter celebration?

➡ Would you rather spend Easter at the top of the tallest skyscraper or stuck at the top of a Ferris wheel?

➡ Would you rather go bungee jumping off a tall bridge or ride the tallest roller coaster, which also goes upside down, on Easter?

→ Would you rather get to choose the menu for your Easter meal all by yourself or have your whole family help decide?

→ Would you rather discover an island on Earth that you can only visit on Easter or be able to live on another planet all year?

→ Would you rather have to view everything through binoculars or a magnifying glass on Easter day?

→ Would you rather sail on a pirate ship but not discover treasure on Easter or use a metal detector in the hot sun on the beach and find gold?

→ Would you rather your favorite author releases a new book on Easter or your favorite band releases a new album?

→ Would you rather spend Easter underwater in a submarine or spend Easter underwater breathing through gills?

→ Would you rather paint your whole house Easter colors or paint the front door of your house to look like an Easter egg?

→ Would you rather only be able to whisper on Easter or have to say everything in your loudest voice?

→ Would you rather spend Easter at the International Space Station or be able to visit outer space for an entire month?

SPRING AND SPRING BREAK

➡ Would you rather have as many legs as a caterpillar or have wings like a butterfly?

➡ Would you rather be able to fly like a ladybug or roll up like a roly-poly?

➡ Would you rather have to take care of a hutch full of rabbits or a beehive?

➡ Would you rather run around trying to catch a squirrel or hop around trying to catch a frog?

➡ Would you rather be able to fly like a bird or swim like a fish?

→ Would you rather have a yard full of concrete or a yard full of real grass?

→ Would you rather play Duck, Duck, Goose with your friends or challenge them to a duck waddle race?

→ Would you rather play leapfrog or Red Rover with your friends?

→ Would you rather roll down a big grassy hill or fly a huge kite on a windy day?

→ Would you rather hang glide or skydive?

→ Would you rather ride in a hot air balloon or a helicopter?

→ Would you rather wear earplugs in the swimming pool or a nose plug?

→ Would you rather read one page from your diary in front of your class before spring break or show them a video of an embarrassing moment?

→ Would you rather plant spring flowers or dig up worms?

→ Would you rather spend spring break on the beach or in the mountains?

→ Would you rather go someplace hot or cold for spring break?

→ Would you rather have a jump rope contest or hula hoop contest on spring break?

→ Would you rather have to hopscotch or leapfrog when you walk anywhere on spring break?

→ Would you rather spend spring break watching new animals being born or new flowers blooming in the garden?

→ Would you rather be a chick hatching from an egg or a plant bursting out of a seed?

→ Would you rather be a flower blossom or a leaf on a tree?

→ Would you rather be a flower that grows in a yard or one that lives by the side of the road?

SPRING AND SPRING BREAK

69

→ Would you rather be grass growing on a school playground or under a park bench?

→ Would you rather jump in a puddle of mud or a puddle of rain?

→ Would you rather wear rain boots that are two sizes too big or one size too small?

→ Would you rather be caught in the rain barefoot or in your bathing suit?

→ Would you rather get caught in the rain in your pajamas or your school clothes?

→ Would you rather wear rain boots that are too big or have your umbrella blow away?

→ Would you rather get caught in spring rain or a winter snowstorm?

→ Would you rather splash in a rain puddle or jump into a pile of snow?

→ Would you rather hold a worm or a tadpole in your bare hands?

→ Would you rather raise a caterpillar as it turns into a butterfly or a tadpole as it turns into a frog?

→ Would you rather swim in a pond full of ducks or a pond full of frogs?

→ Would you rather find a bird's nest or a beehive in your yard?

→ Would you rather live in a bird's nest or in a beehive if you could shrink yourself down?

→ Would you rather eat bugs like a baby bird or eat nuts like a baby squirrel?

➜ Would you rather plant a garden full of flowers or vegetables?

➜ Would you rather live in a place where all year round it feels like spring or like fall?

➜ Would you rather migrate somewhere else for winter or stay in your house all year?

➜ Would you rather climb a tree or fly a kite?

➜ Would you rather paint a picture or make a sculpture out of clay?

→ Would you rather make slime or bake cookies?

→ Would you rather watch three episodes of your favorite show or one movie?

→ Would you rather play a video game with your parents or a board game with your friends?

→ Would you rather go outside to play at recess when it is raining or stay dry inside?

→ Would you rather get an hour for recess at school or 30 minutes to play video games?

➜ Would you rather play kickball against your friends or play baseball on the same team as your enemies on spring break?

➜ Would you rather go see a movie or go to a concert on spring break?

➜ Would you rather run everywhere or skip everywhere on spring break?

➜ Would you rather go see a baseball game or a basketball game on spring break?

→ Would you rather go fishing or have a picnic outside on spring break?

→ Would you rather grill hot dogs or grill hamburgers on spring break?

→ Would you rather jump on a trampoline or jump in a bounce house on spring break?

→ Would you rather ride in a four-wheeler or drive a go-kart on spring break?

→ Would you rather roller skate or skateboard for the entire spring break?

SPRING AND SPRING BREAK

➡ Would you rather ride a bike or a scooter in the school halls on the day before spring break?

➡ Would you rather catch a butterfly in a net or dress up like a butterfly every day over spring break?

➡ Would you rather catch enough butterflies or enough lightning bugs to fill a jar on spring break?

➡ Would you rather play baseball with your friends or ride your bike all alone over spring break?

WOULD YOU RATHER FOR KIDS EASTER EDITION

→ Would you rather have the power to make it rain whenever you wanted or to make flowers grow whenever you wanted in spring?

→ Would you rather spend three hours outside grilling food or planting a garden in spring?

→ Would you rather go to the beach or go camping for spring break?

→ Would you rather play with a dolphin or a penguin on your spring break vacation?

→ Would you rather go to the zoo or the aquarium on spring break?

→ Would you rather go to an amusement park or a water park on spring break?

→ Would you rather visit a new museum every day or just one art gallery during spring break?

→ Would you rather be invisible or be able to fly for your entire spring break?

→ Would you rather eat only hamburgers or only pizza on spring break?

→ Would you rather be able to play only inside or only outside for the whole spring break?

→ Would you rather have a broken arm or a broken leg over spring break?

WOULD YOU RATHER FOR KIDS EASTER EDITION

→ Would you rather trip in front of your whole class on the last day of school or have a splinter in your thumb for all of spring break?

→ Would you rather bring home the class pet bird or class pet hamster over spring break?

→ Would you rather your only snack on spring break be chips or popcorn?

→ Would you rather eat only hot dogs or only tacos for school lunch the week before spring break?

➜ Would you rather it be really hot during all of spring break or rain for half of spring break?

➜ Would you rather sing all of your words or talk like a pirate during spring break?

➜ Would you rather eat popsicles or ice cream for spring break treats?

➜ Would you rather surf in the ocean or build a sandcastle on your spring break beach vacation?

WOULD YOU RATHER FOR KIDS EASTER EDITION

→ Would you rather be a squirrel or a frog during spring break?

→ Would you rather make money by holding a garage sale or running a lemonade stand during spring break?

→ Would you rather go on a day-long hike or go on a three-mile bike ride every day during spring break?

→ Would you rather catch a frog and enter it in a jumping contest or build a kite and enter it in a kite-flying contest over spring break?

SPRING AND SPRING BREAK

➡️ Would you rather do homework or do your chores on spring break?

➡️ Would you rather come up with your own card game or design your own board game over spring break?

➡️ Would you rather stay up late every night or go on an adventure every day during spring break?

➡️ Would you rather watch a movie every night or eat ice cream for dessert every day during spring break?

➡️ Would you rather vacuum the entire house or clean out the garage over spring break?

➡️ Would you rather sleep late every day or eat a big breakfast every morning during spring break?

➡️ Would you rather play video games for two hours a day or play outside all day during spring break?

➡️ Would you rather get a new bike or a new video game to play over spring break?

BEFORE YOU GO...

Did you have fun with those sometimes corny, sometimes silly Would You Rather questions?

Now that you have gotten the hang of it, spend some time thinking up your own Would You Rather questions! To make them extra thought-provoking, customize your questions according to family traditions or fun things you do with your friends

Remember to make the game even more fun by asking people to share their reasons behind why they chose one option over another. Often hearing the reasons why is the most fun part of the game because you learn how people think!

If you want to make this game a tradition, consider keeping score so you can look back on it for years to come.

You can also play Would You Rather games for any holiday, celebration, or theme. Think about any characters or traditions that are involved with the holiday and you will be able to come up with more questions.

With Easter, you can come up with questions about the Easter Bunny, Easter baskets, Easter traditions, the fun you can have at Easter celebrations, the food you eat for Easter, and the candy you get in your Easter baskets.

Once you think of the questions, you can play the game anywhere! It is great to play on long road trips, at school or even when you are waiting in line at the grocery store.

Would You Rather questions are even fun to ask when you are meeting new people or if you cannot think of anything to talk about.

Have fun coming up with your own questions, getting to know each other and being as silly as possible!

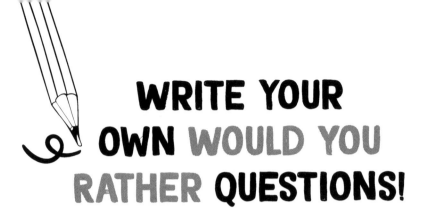

WRITE YOUR OWN WOULD YOU RATHER QUESTIONS!

Have fun coming up with your own questions to play with your friends and family!

WOULD YOU RATHER FOR KIDS EASTER EDITION

WOULD YOU RATHER FOR KIDS EASTER EDITION

REFERENCES

icebreakers.ws. (n.d.). Would You Rather? Game. Icebreakers Ideas Games Activities! Retrieved February 20, 2021, from https://www.icebreakers.ws/small-group/would-you-rather-game.html

Made in the USA
Middletown, DE
26 March 2021